HOW TO REAP YOUR HARVEST

GLORIA COPELAND and PASTOR GEORGE PEARSONS

For more information about Kenneth Copeland Ministries, visit kcm.org or call 1-800-600-7395 (U.S. only) or +1-817-852-6000.

ISBN 978-1-57562-626-0
#30-0831

Unless otherwise noted, all scripture is from the *King James Version* of the Bible.

HOW TO REAP YOUR HARVEST

GLORIA COPELAND and
PASTOR GEORGE PEARSONS

TABLE OF CONTENTS

The Missing Link

DAY 1

A. Matthew 9:37—The harvest truly is plenteous, but the laborers are few.

1. MSG: "'What a huge harvest!' he said to his disciples. 'How few workers!'"

2. On Sept. 28, 1999, Keith Moore said concerning EMIC's giving:

God's heart is grieved. It is bothering God that we are not reaping. Some are disillusioned and aggravated with God. "How much more can I give?" You think you are waiting on God. You think reaping is automatic. You think once you put the money in, it's all up to Him. You just sit back and relax and think it's all going to just come on you. That is ignorance and confusion. I challenge you to hear the word of the Lord and make up your mind and say, "I am not just a good giver. I am a good reaper. I am going to get real good at reaping."

3. It would be wrong for a farmer to leave a harvest standing in the field.

   a. Pop's peaches

   b. "If you want to taste it, you have to harvest it."
      —Gloria Copeland

   c. The same principle applies to us.

4. It is time for us to get up, get out to our fields and reap our harvests.

   a. "When harvest time comes, you'd better call it in!"
      —Gloria Copeland

5. Jeremiah 17:7-8 (MSG): "But blessed is the man who trusts me, God, the woman who sticks with God. They're like trees replanted in Eden, putting down roots near the rivers—never a worry through the hottest of summers, never dropping a leaf, serene and calm through droughts, bearing fresh fruit every season."

a. "Once you harvest, it's not seasonal—it's continual."
—Gloria Copeland

B. Reaping: The Missing Link to Increase

1. My immediate challenge to the church:
    a. We are not just good givers.
    b. We are good reapers.
    c. We are going to "get real good at reaping."

2. I studied Keith Moore's series, *Rules of Reaping.*

3. I conducted a three-day seminar at church.

4. We called in the harvest every time we sowed.

5. Result: We have become much better reapers.

C. Psalm 107:36-37—It Is Time to Reap Our Harvest!

1. NLT-96: "He brings the hungry to settle there and build their cities. They sow their fields, plant their vineyards, and harvest their bumper crops."

2. MSG: "[He] brought in the hungry and settled them there; they moved in—what a great place to live! They sowed the fields, they planted vineyards, they reaped a bountiful harvest."

3. THEY sowed—THEY planted—THEY reaped.
    a. "You pick it, you pack it, you ship it." —Gloria Copeland

4. Verse 38 (MSG): "He blessed them and they prospered greatly; their herds of cattle never decreased."

5. Goal of this series: We are going to "get real good at reaping"!

If you haven't thought of yourself as a harvester before now, start thinking of yourself that way. Renew your mind to the truth of God's Word. Dare to believe the Lord of the Harvest is calling you—yes, you!—to help Him bring in His end-time crops. He's speaking to you and saying, *Until now, you've known Me as the Lord over your seed. You've known Me as your bread provider. But I want you to know Me now as Lord and Minister of the harvest.*

—From "Get Your Mind on the Harvest" by Kenneth Copeland

NOTES

NOTES

Created to Harvest

DAY 2

A. Matthew 9:37—The harvest truly is plenteous, but the laborers are few.

    1. On Sept. 28, 1999, Keith Moore said concerning EMIC's giving:

> God's heart is grieved. It is bothering God that we are not reaping. Some are disillusioned and aggravated with God. "How much more can I give?" You think you are waiting on God. You think reaping is automatic. You think once you put the money in, it's all up to Him. You just sit back and relax and think it's all going to just come on you. That is ignorance and confusion. I challenge you to hear the word of the Lord and make up your mind and say, "I am not just a good giver. I am a good reaper. I am going to get real good at reaping."

    2. The principle of reaping was the missing link to our increase.

    3. I immersed myself in Keith Moore's *Rules of Reaping* series.

    4. I conducted a three-day seminar at church.

    5. Result: We have become much better reapers.

B. We Were Created by God to Reap the Harvest

    1. Reaping is not a new concept—it is the primary element of THE BLESSING.

    2. Genesis 1:28: "And God blessed them, and God said unto them, Be fruitful, and multiply...."

        a. "Any time is sowing time." —Gloria Copeland

    3. Genesis 1:29 (NLT): "Then God said, 'Look! I have given you every seed-bearing plant throughout the earth and all the fruit trees for your food.'"

      a.   There is a harvest attached to every seed.

4.   Genesis 2:8-9 (MSG): "Then God planted a garden in Eden, in the east. He put the Man he had just made in it. God made all kinds of trees grow from the ground, trees beautiful to look at and good to eat."

5.   Genesis 2:15-16 (NIV): "The Lord God took the man and put him in the Garden of Eden to work it and take care of it. And the Lord God commanded the man, 'You are free to eat from any tree in the garden.'"

      a.   "We still have a harvesting gene. It's in our DNA." —Gloria Copeland

      b.   There is a difference between natural harvest and spiritual harvest. The spiritual harvest does not rot (spoil)—it is still out there waiting to be harvested.

C. Genesis 8:22—The Law of Seedtime and Harvest

1.   NLT: "As long as the earth remains, there will be planting and harvest, cold and heat, summer and winter, day and night."

      a.   *Harvest* (HEB) = the process of harvesting; what is reaped

2.   Matthew 6:24-26—We are better than birds because we were created by God to sow and reap.

      a.   Birds don't sow—but we do.

      b.   Birds don't reap—but we do.

      c.   Birds don't gather into barns—but we do.

3.   Proverbs 3:9-10: "Honour the Lord with thy substance, and with the firstfruits of all thine increase: so shall thy barns be filled with plenty, and thy presses shall burst out with new wine."

That's the way we, as seed-sowing believers, ought to be today. We should have our "reaping" faith in gear and our minds on the harvest. That's a switch for a lot of us because until now, we've focused our faith primarily on planting. We've concentrated on God's promise to provide seed to the sower and bread to the eater. Thank God for such bread-receiving, seed-sowing faith! It's wonderful. It's opened the door for God to meet our needs and give us enough to invest in the work of His kingdom. But that's not all God wants to do for us. He didn't just promise to give us food to eat and seed to sow, He promised to multiply that seed and give us a harvest.

—From "Get Your Mind on the Harvest" by Kenneth Copeland

NOTES

NOTES

Rules of Reaping

DAY 3

A. Proverbs 10:5—Reaping Is Not Automatic

1. TLB: "A wise youth makes hay while the sun shines, but what a shame to see a lad who sleeps away his hour of opportunity."

    a. *Opportunity* and *reaping* are synonymous.

2. MSG: "Go fishing during harvest—that's stupid."

3. Harvesting takes effort on our part.

    a. We must not sleep through our harvest.

        i. "You can't sleep and harvest at the same time."
            —Gloria Copeland

    b. We must not allow our harvest to stand in the field.

4. Proverbs 6:6-8 (MSG): "You lazy fool, look at an ant. Watch it closely; let it teach you a thing or two. Nobody has to tell it what to do. All summer it stores up food; at harvest it stockpiles provisions."

5. Galatians 6:7: "Be not deceived; God is not mocked: for whatsoever a man soweth, that shall HE also reap."

    a. "A man decides his harvest by the kind of seed he sows. Exact seed is exact harvest." —Gloria Copeland

    b. "We reap with our words." —Gloria Copeland

B. Mark 4:26-29—Reaping Is Our Responsibility

1. Verse 29 (MSG): "When the grain is fully formed, he reaps—harvest time!"

2. Who did the sowing? The man.

3. Who did the growing? God.

4. Who reaped the harvest? The man.

5. "Jesus compared the kingdom of God with the planting of seed and reaping the harvest. It's a simple concept. One all of us understand. Why, then, aren't all of us producing bumper crops every season? Because we are sitting around waiting for God to do all the work." —Kenneth Copeland, *From Faith to Faith*

    a. The harvest doesn't jump from the field to the barn.

    b. We have to go get it.

C. Ecclesiastes 11:4—Reaping Requires Faith

1. AMPC: "He who observes the wind [and waits for all conditions to be favorable] will not sow, and he who regards the clouds will not reap."

2. NLT: "Farmers who wait for perfect weather never plant. If they watch every cloud, they never harvest."

3. People who continually look at negative conditions become discouraged and will fail to sow and reap.

4. Galatians 6:9 (MSG): "So let's not allow ourselves to get fatigued doing good. At the right time we will harvest a good crop if we don't give up, or quit."

5. Genesis 26:12 (NIV): "Isaac planted crops in that land and the same year reaped a hundredfold, because the Lord blessed him."

    a. We continually harvest—even during the toughest times.

    b. Jeremiah 17:7-8 (NLT): "But blessed are those who trust in the Lord and have made the Lord their hope and confidence. They are like trees planted along a riverbank, with roots that reach deep into the water. Such trees are not bothered by the heat or worried by long months of drought. Their leaves stay green, and they never stop producing fruit."

NOTES

NOTES

Tithing and Reaping

DAY 4

A. Proverbs 3:9-10—A Successful Harvester Tithes

1. NKJV: "<u>Honor</u> the Lord with your possessions, _{SUBSTANCE} and with the firstfruits of all your increase; so your barns will be filled ~~with plenty~~ TO OVERFLOWING, and your vats will overflow with new wine."

2. Tithing is not sowing.

   a. Tithing is returning to the Lord what is His.

   b. It is returning to the Lord the firstfruits of your increase.

   c. The tithe belongs to Him.

3. Tithing is honoring God with His 10 percent.

4. Leviticus 27:30 (NKJV): "And all the tithe of the land, *whether* of the seed of the land *or* of the fruit of the tree, *is* the Lord's. It *is* holy to the Lord."

5. People don't reap because they don't tithe.

   a. "When you tithe, you're bringing God into your deal."
   —Gloria Copeland

B. Malachi 3:10-11—Tithing Protects Our Harvest

1. Tithing is the key to your seed being blessed.

   a. "When you tithe, you bring God into your deal."
   —Gloria Copeland

2. Verse 10—He opens the windows of heaven and sends the rain on the seed that you have sown.

3. Verse 11: "And I will rebuke the devourer (seed eaters, crop-destroying pests) for your sakes, and he shall not destroy (corrupt, spoil or ruin) the fruits of your ground; neither shall your vine cast her fruit before the time in the field."

4. Verse 11 (NIV-84): "'I will prevent pests from devouring your crops, and the vines in your fields will not cast their fruit,' says the Lord Almighty."

5. Verse 11 (NLT): "'Your crops will be abundant, for I will guard them from insects and disease. Your grapes will not fall from the vine before they are ripe,' says the Lord of Heaven's Armies."

C. A Farmer's Experiment in Tithing

From a book written in 1940 by a farmer named Perry Hayden

Perry Hayden heard his pastor preach a message about tithing. He decided to try an experiment to see how much harvest a seed would produce.

His plan was to sow 1 cubic inch of wheat—360 kernels. He committed to the Lord that, for a period of six years, he would tithe 10 percent of the harvest and sow the rest.

In the first year, it took a 4-foot by 8-foot plot of land to sow 1 cubic inch of seed. At harvest time, he scraped the ground to get every kernel of wheat. Every precious seed counted. The first year produced a fiftyfold harvest.

He tithed 10 percent.

In the second year, it took a 24-foot by 60-foot plot of land to sow the seed from the harvest of the first year. He tithed 10 percent.

In the third year, it took three-quarters of an acre to sow. He tithed 10 percent.

In the fourth year, it took 14 acres to sow. He tithed 10 percent.

In the fifth year, it took 230 acres to sow. He tithed 10 percent.

By the sixth year, it took over 2600 acres to sow 5,000 bushels.

Three hundred sixty kernels had turned into 55 billion. And the largest yield was only fiftyfold. Perry Hayden made $288,000 in six years, compared to the other farmers who only made an average of $21,000.

The experiment worked. God can bless your harvest when you tithe.

Tithing is the open door to THE BLESSING, and it's THE BLESSING that God set forth that's going to meet your needs, give you what

you need, bless you, keep you well, keep you prosperous. Our tithing opens that door for God to move supernaturally. Tithing keeps the door open when you do it in faith. Now you can tithe in unbelief and it's not the same. But, when you tithe in faith, you worship God with your tithe. Ken and I pray over our tithe. We worship God with it. We believe God, and we sow it to the kingdom of God.

—Gloria Copeland

MAL 3:8-12 (AMP) Will a man rob or defraud god?
Yet you rob and defraud Me.
But you say, In what way do we rob + defraud You?
You have with held your tithes + offerings

vs 9 You are cursed with the curse, For you
are robbing Me - even this whole nation.
                    FIRST   TENTH PART
vs 10 Bring all the tithes (the whole 10ᵗʰ of your income)
                                          MEAT
into the storehouse that there may be food in my house
         PLACE WHERE YOU ARE SP. FED   PLENTY AND LACK TO CARRY ON THE WORK
and prove Me now by it says the Lord of hosts
   TEST EXAMINE INVESTIGATE TRY
      · If I will not open the windows of heaven
                         UNSTOP   FLOODGATES GEN 7:11 8:2
      For you and pour you out a blessing
              EMPTY OUT   ABUNDANT LIBERAL PROSP
      that there shall not be room enough to
      receive it. OVERFLOW
                 CRIPPLE PARALYZE TORMENT   SEEDEATER
      · vs 11 And I will rebuke the devourer
         (insects + plagues - seedeaters) For your sakes
      · he shall not destroy the Fruits of your
         ground
                              MISCARRY-
      · neither shall your vine drop its fruit
         before the time in the field says the
         Lord of Hosts
      · vs 12 And all nations shall call you
         happy and blessed For you shall be a
         land of delight says the Lord of Hosts

(NLT) I will open the windows of heaven For you.
      I will pour out a blessing so great you
      wont have enough room to take it in.
      Try it! Let me prove it to you! Your crops
      will be abundant, For I will guard them
      From insects and disease. Your grapes
      will not shrivel before they ripe. All
      nations will call you blessed For your
      land will be such a delight.
(LAMSA) We shall surely shout "We cant u! We
      cant hold anymore!"

Tithe = an act of obedience + love
It is a covenant thing

v.8 "I wouldn't steal from God under
any circumstances" KC

13 - How not to receive
18 Lord listens

MALACHI 4   Infidelity of the people. The promise of blessing

[a] he *is* like a refiner's fire, and like fullers' soap:

3 And he shall sit *as* a refiner and purifier of silver: and he shall purify the sons of Levi, and purge them as gold and silver, that they may offer unto the LORD an offering in righteousness.

4 Then shall [d] the offering of Judah and Jerusalem be pleasant unto the LORD, as in the days of old, and as in [1] former years.

5 And I will come near to you to judgment; and I will be a swift witness against the sorcerers, and against the adulterers, and against false swearers, and against [f] those that [4] oppress the hireling in his wages, [g] the widow, and the fatherless, and [h] that turn aside the stranger *from his right*, and fear not me, saith the LORD of hosts.

6 For I *am* the LORD, [i] I change not; [j] therefore ye sons of Jacob are not consumed. *order*

7 ¶ [k] Even from the days of your fathers ye are gone away from mine ordinances, and have not kept *them*. [m] Return unto me, and I will return unto you, saith the LORD of hosts. [n] But ye said, Wherein shall we return? 8 ¶ Will a man rob God? Yet ye have robbed me. But ye say, Wherein have we robbed thee? In [p] tithes and offerings.

9 Ye *are* cursed with a curse: for ye have robbed me, even this whole nation.

10 Bring ye all the tithes into the storehouse, that there may be [r] meat in mine house, and [s] prove me now herewith, saith the LORD of hosts, if I will not open you the windows of heaven, and [t] pour you out a blessing, that *there shall* not be room enough *to receive it.*

11 And I will rebuke [u] the devourer for your sakes, and he shall not [8] destroy the fruits of your ground; neither [x] shall your

Marginal references (center column)
a Isa. 4. 4.
Mt. 3. 11, 12.
b Lk. 1. 48.
c ch. 2. 17. Ps 78:17-22
d ch. 1. 11.
1 Or, *ancient*.
e Job 21. 7. Jer. 12. 1. Zeph. 1. 12.
2 Heb. *observation*.
3 Heb. *in black*.
f Lev. 19. 13.
4 Or, *defraud*.
g Deu. 24. 17.
5 Heb. *are built.*
h Ex. 23. 6.
i Jas. 1. 17.
j Lam. 3. 22. Am. 9. 9. & 149. 9. Dan. 7. 10. Rev. 20. 12.
l Ac. 7. 51.
m Zech. 1. 3.
n ch. 1. 6.
6 Or, *special treasure.* Ex. 19. 5. 1 Pe. 2. 9. o Ps. 103. 13.
p Ne. 13. 10, 12.
q Ps. 58. 10, 11 & 73. 17-20.
r Ps. 111. 5.
s ch. 3. 2.
t 2 Co. 9. 6-8.
u 2 Th. 1. 8.
v Isa. 47. 14.
7 Heb. *Empty out.*
w Mt. 3. 10. Lk. 3. 9.
8 Heb. *corrupt.*
x Jer. 8. 13. y Ps. 84. 11. Lk. 1. 78. Jn. 1. 4, 9 & 12. 46. 2 Pe. 1. 19. Rev. 2. 28.

Right column

vine cast her fruit before the time in the field, saith the LORD of hosts. *= livelihood*

12 And [b] all nations shall call you blessed: for ye shall be a delightsome land, saith the LORD of hosts.

13 ¶ [c] Your words have been stout against me, saith the LORD. Yet ye say, What have we spoken *so much* against thee?

14 [e] Ye have said, It *is* vain to serve God: and what profit *is it* that we have kept his [2] ordinance, and that we have walked [3] mournfully before the LORD of hosts?

15 And now we call the proud happy; yea, they that work wickedness [5] are set up; yea, *they that* tempt God are even delivered.

16 ¶ Then they that feared the LORD spake often one to another; and the LORD hearkened, and heard *it*, and [k] a book of remembrance was written before him for them that feared the LORD, and that thought upon his name. *the Lord hears*

17 And they shall be mine, saith the LORD of hosts, in that day when I make up my [6] jewels; and I will spare them, [o] as a man spareth his own son that serveth him. *NLT = judgment*

18 Then shall ye return, and [q] discern between the righteous and the wicked, between him that serveth God and him that serveth him not. *Is 3:10*

CHAPTER 4

FOR, behold, [s] the day cometh, [u] that shall burn as an oven; and all the proud, yea, and all that do wickedly, [v] shall be stubble: and [w] the day that cometh shall burn them up, saith the LORD of hosts, that it shall leave them neither root nor branch.

2 ¶ But unto you that fear my name shall [y] the Sun of right-

1108

Right margin handwritten
Who stops ones words
v.17 2:17
AMP
Ps 78
Deut 1- murmur
Ez
who
NLT
Ez 33 NLT
T647

Left margin handwritten

Ex 23:6 Amp
You shall not pervert the justice due to four poor in his cause.
James 5:4
"Thou shalt not offend/pervert the justice due to poor"
James 1:13-17

Give tithe Gen 15:20

Zech 5:3 thief
Elevated city Josh 6:17?
Lev 27:30-31
V. 9 = overflow

who robbed God
Josh 6+7

2 Kings 4:6
2 Tim 2:20
Windows = Deut 28:12
PRV 20:26
Brim = until there is none left in heaven. Limitlessness pt. Psalm

windows = floodgates
a flood of blessings flood can't be contained. Don't try to contain it, let it go through you.

It will pour out until there is no more in heaven. If necessary He will create more. empty out ↑ margin

Bottom handwritten

v.11 tithe protects the harvest.

meat = provision
blessing wall
God is saying, connect with me. I want to connect to you.

devourer = seed eater

v. 8 who robbed God caused curse

Lord of hosts = Lord of all of His armies & He will use them for whatever He needs. Has to do with His sovereignty. Will do whatever it takes.

to them that fear God. Elijah's coming and office   MALACHI 4

eousness arise with healing in his wings; and ye shall go forth, and grow up as calves of the stall.

3 And ye shall tread down the wicked; for they shall be ashes under the soles of your feet in the day that I shall do *this*, saith the LORD of hosts.

4 ¶ Remember ye *the law of Moses my servant, which I commanded unto him *in Hôr′-ĕb for

a ch. 3. 1.
b Mt. 11. 14.
c Joel 2. 31.

d Lk. 1. 17.

e Ex. 20. 3, &c.
f Deu. 4. 10.

all Israel, *with* the statutes and judgments.

5 ¶ *a*Behold, I will send you *b*E-lī′-jäh the prophet *c*before the coming of the great and dreadful day of the LORD:

6 And he shall *d*turn the heart of the fathers to the children, and the heart of the children to their fathers, lest I come and smite the earth with a curse.

Tithe connects you up to your deliverance
Tithe connects to your God + His Covenant
Tithe is all about honor. mal 3:5   Prov 3:9-10

THE END OF THE PROPHETS.

v. 8 Tithes and offerings:
Can't give a right offering until you give the tenth
(Like borrowing car and paying back $20 a week - Don't
Want your $20 I want my car.) Cuflo
Have to see keeping tithe as transgression of covenant

Joshua 6, 7, 8

Refusing to tithe disconnects from covenant of blessing

Tithe for the future Deut 14:22 = tithe of seed   eat before Lord
* Tithe that you learn to reverence the Lord. Deut 14:23

mal
v. 13-14 "They began to doubt the character of God and they
robbed God." Nel. B. note 792

Ps 111:45   covenant thing. You are honoring God
(Amp)   recognizing Him as your provider.
"He will remember His covenant forever and
imprint it on his mind. 45

Prov 11:24   Scatter = increase   withholding = poverty
sowing   = seed grows =

NOTES

NOTES

Sowing and Reaping

DAY 5

A. Galatians 6:7—A Successful Harvester Sows Seed

1. NKJV: "Do not be deceived, God is not mocked; for whatever a man sows, that he will also reap."

2. AMPC: "Do not be deceived and deluded and misled; God will not allow Himself to be sneered at (scorned, disdained, or mocked by mere pretensions or professions, or by His precepts being set aside.) [He inevitably deludes himself who attempts to delude God.] For whatever a man sows, that and that only is what he will reap."

3. It is not, "reaping and sowing"—it is "sowing and reaping."

4. In order to reap a harvest, you must sow a seed.

5. God will even minister seed to the sower.

   a. If you don't have anything, just ask God for seed and He will get you started.

   b. Brother Copeland sowed a pencil in Oral Roberts' partner offering.

6. Every seed is attached to a harvest.

7. "Everything takes faith for manifestation." —Gloria Copeland

B. 2 Corinthians 9:6-8—Qualities of a Good Sower

1. AMPC: "[Remember] this: he who sows sparingly and grudgingly will also reap sparingly and grudgingly, and he who sows generously [that blessings may come to someone] will also reap generously and with blessings. Let each one [give] as he has made up his own mind and purposed in his heart, not reluctantly or sorrowfully or under compulsion, for God loves (He takes pleasure in, prizes above other things, and is unwilling to abandon or to do without) a cheerful (joyous, "prompt to do it") giver [whose heart is in his giving]. And God is able to make all grace (every favor and earthly blessing) come to you in abundance, so that you may always and under all circumstances and whatever the need be self-sufficient [possessing enough to require no aid or support and furnished in abundance for every good work and charitable donation]."

2. Verse 6—*Generous* (Proverbs 11:24-25—Liberal giver)

3. Verse 7—*Spirit-led* (JBP—Let everyone give as his heart tells him)

4. Verse 7—*Obedient* (Isaiah 1:19—willing and obedient)

5. Verse 7—*Cheerful* (AMPC—Joyous, prompt to do it giver)

6. Verse 8—*Result* (AMPC—Furnished in abundance for every good work)

C. Keys to Sowing

1. Sow into the areas you desire to reap a harvest.
    a. Money, clothes, houses, cars, rest, help
    b. Every seed produces after its own kind.

2. If you really believe in sowing and reaping, get busy finding something to sow.

3. Ask, "What increases are we going to make in our sowing?"

4. Don't forget where you sowed.
    a. Check the field all the time.

5. Sow into good ground and you will have a much bigger harvest.

NOTES

Harvest Essentials—Part 1

DAY 6

A. Previous Week's Review

1. The Missing Link

   a. Keith Moore said concerning EMIC's giving, "God's heart is grieved. It is bothering God that we are not reaping. I challenge you to hear the word of the Lord and make up your mind and say, "I am not just a good giver. I am a good reaper. I am going to get real good at reaping."
   —Keith Moore, Sept. 28, 1999

   b. Reaping: The missing link to our increase

   c. Result: We have become much better reapers.

2. We were created by God to reap harvest.

   a. "If you want to taste it, you have to harvest it."
   —Gloria Copeland

   b. "We still have a harvesting gene. It's in our DNA."
   —Gloria Copeland

3. Rules of Reaping:

   a. Reaping is not automatic.

   b. Reaping is our responsibility.

   c. Reaping requires faith.

4. "If you haven't thought of yourself as a harvester, start thinking of yourself that way."
   —From "Get Your Mind on the Harvest" by Kenneth Copeland

5. The connection between tithing and reaping

6. The connection between sowing and reaping

B. Mark 4:26-29—Three Essentials for a Great Harvest

Quotes by Kenneth Copeland, *From Faith to Faith*

1. "Jesus compared the kingdom of God with the planting of seed and reaping the harvest. It's a simple concept. One all of us understand.

2. "Why, then, aren't all of us producing bumper crops every season?

3. "Because we are sitting around waiting for God to do all the work.

4. "He doesn't operate that way. He'll work with you, but He won't do it all.

5. "There are some essential things you must do by faith if you want to have a crop to reap at harvest time."

C. Essential #1—Expect Your Seed to Grow

1. "First, you must sow the seed of the Word in faith, expecting it to grow."
   —Kenneth Copeland, *From Faith to Faith*

2. Live in a continual state of expectation of your seed producing harvest.

3. Luke 6:38 (ESV): "Give, and IT WILL be given to you."

4. "I am expecting a record-breaking harvest."

5. Psalm 65:11 (NLT): "You crown the year with a bountiful harvest; even the hard pathways overflow with abundance."

I am expecting my greatest blessing and my greatest harvest ever, today—because great grace is upon us all.

NOTES

NOTES

Harvest Essentials—Part 2

DAY 7

A. Mark 4:26-29—Three Essentials for a Great Harvest

Quotes by Kenneth Copeland, *From Faith to Faith*

1. "Jesus compared the kingdom of God with the planting of seed and reaping the harvest. It's a simple concept. One all of us understand.

2. "Why, then, aren't all of us producing bumper crops every season?

3. "Because we are sitting around waiting for God to do all the work.

4. "He doesn't operate that way. He'll work with you, but He won't do it all.

5. "There are some essential things you must do by faith if you want to have a crop to reap at harvest time."

B. Essential #1—Expect Your Seed to Grow

1. "First, you must sow the seed of the Word in faith, expecting it to grow."
   —Kenneth Copeland, *From Faith to Faith*

2. Live in a continual state of expectation of your seed producing harvest.

3. Luke 6:38 (ESV): "Give, and IT WILL be given to you."

4. "I am expecting a record-breaking harvest."

5. Psalm 65:11 (NLT): "You crown the year with a bountiful harvest; even the hard pathways overflow with abundance."

C. Essential #2—Water Your Seed

1. "Water it every day with praise. Water it with the spiritual water of the Word. That Word contains life and those seed promises can't grow without it." —Kenneth Copeland, *From Faith to Faith*

2. Psalm 67:5-6: "Let the people praise thee, O God; let all the people praise thee. Then shall the earth yield her increase; and God, even our own God, shall bless us."

   a. Note the connection between praise and harvest.

   b. Praise is like "Miracle Gro®"—it moves things along.

   c. The depth of your praise will determine the magnitude of your harvest.

   d. Praise gives voice to your faith, expressing your utmost confidence in God's Word.

3. "Praise God, my seed always produces a bumper crop."

4. "Thank You, Lord—the hundredfold return is working for me all the time."

5. Galatians 6:9 (AMPC): "Let us not lose heart and grow weary and faint in acting nobly and doing right, for in due time and at the appointed season WE SHALL REAP, if we do not loosen and relax our courage and faint."

You have to sow with the Word. You have to reap with the Word. You add your words of faith to His words of faith until the manifestation of the fruit appears (the car, the healing, the house, the finances, the supply, the peace).

—Gloria Copeland

NOTES

NOTES

Harvest Essentials—Part 3

DAY 8

A. Mark 4:26-29—Three Essentials for a Great Harvest

Quotes by Kenneth Copeland, *From Faith to Faith*

1. "Jesus compared the kingdom of God with the planting of seed and reaping the harvest. It's a simple concept. One all of us understand.

2. "Why, then, aren't all of us producing bumper crops every season?

3. "Because we are sitting around waiting for God to do all the work.

4. "He doesn't operate that way. He'll work with you, but He won't do it all.

5. "There are some essential things you must do by faith if you want to have a crop to reap at harvest time."

B. Review of the First Two Essentials

Quotes by Kenneth Copeland, *From Faith to Faith*

1. Essential #1—Expect Your Seed to Grow
   a. "First, you must sow the seed of the Word in faith, expecting it to grow."
   b. Live in a continual state of expectation of your seed producing a record-breaking harvest.

2. Essential #2—Water Your Seed
   a. "Water it every day with praise. Water it with the spiritual water of the Word. That Word contains life and those seed promises can't grow without it."

b. The depth of your praise will determine the magnitude of your harvest.

C. Essential #3—Keep the Weeds Out

1. "When the weeds of unforgiveness, doubt, fear, discouragement, (and all the other junk the devil tries to sow into your crop) try to enter in, get rid of them. They'll choke the Word. That's going to take some diligence on your part. No one else will do it for you. You're going to have to weed your own crop yourself. So get tough about it. When a little weed pops up, kill it! Don't hang on to it for even a moment. Pull it up by its roots. Spray it with the Word." — Kenneth Copeland, *From Faith to Faith*

2. Genesis 2:15: "And the Lord God took the man, and put him into the garden of Eden to dress it and to keep it."

    a. *Dress* (HEB) = to work it, till it, cultivate it and develop it

    b. *Keep* (HEB) = to put a hedge of thorns around it, to watch over it; to guard, protect, defend and safeguard; bodyguard and gatekeeper

3. You pull up and cast out the "weeds" with your words of faith.

4. Mark 11:22-26—When you stand praying, forgive.

5. I asked our former KCM South Africa director what her thoughts were about Nelson Mandela. She simply said, "Forgave easily."

Unless the seed and the soil come together, no tomato.

—Gloria Copeland

NOTES

NOTES

What Every Good Harvester Must Know

DAY 9

A. John 4:35—A Good Harvester Must Know WHEN to Reap His Harvest

1. MSG: "As you look around right now, wouldn't you say that in about four months it will be time to harvest? Well, I'm telling you to open your eyes and take a good look at what's right in front of you. These Samaritan fields are ripe. It's harvest time!"

    a. The Holy Spirit will show us when the harvest is ready.

    b. "I know exactly when to reap my harvest!"

2. Joy is a major indicator.

    a. Isaiah 9:3 (TLB): "For Israel will again be great, filled with joy like that of reapers when the harvesttime has come."

    b. The closer the harvest, the more excited you become.

3. Exercise patience until the harvest is ready to reap.

    a. Galatians 6:9 (MOF): "Never let us grow tired of doing what is right, for if we do not faint we shall reap our harvest at the opportune season."

    b. Ecclesiastes 3:2 (MSG): "A right time to plant and another to reap."

B. Genesis 26:12—A Good Harvester Must Know WHERE to Reap His Harvest

1. MSG: "Isaac planted crops in THAT LAND and took in a huge harvest. The man got richer and richer by the day until he was very wealthy."

2. Luke 5:1-11—Peter nearly missed his harvest.

  a. Peter sowed his boat to Jesus to allow Him to preach.

  b. Then, Jesus told him to let down the nets for his harvest.

 3. The Lord will show you where your harvest is located.

  a. Opportunities

  b. Expansion

  c. Projects

  d. New jobs

C. Mark 10:29-30—A Good Harvester Must Know to Reap ALL His Harvest

 1. Verse 30: "...But he shall receive an hundredfold now in this time."

 2. *Receive* (GK) = LAMBANO

  a. To seize or take vs. accept something offered

  b. To lay hold of, procure, claim

 3. The hundredfold must be harvested.

 4. Proverbs 27:23: "Be diligent to know the state of thy flocks and look well to thy herds."

  a. Do you know how much you tithed last year?

  b. Do you know how much you sowed last year?

 5. Reap ALL of your harvest.

  a. It is still out there.

  b. Go get it ALL!

DON'T EAT YOUR HARVEST BEFORE IT'S RIPE

FROM *THE BLESSING OF THE LORD MAKES RICH AND HE ADDS NO SORROW WITH IT* BY KENNETH COPELAND

When Jesus talked about the time of harvest in the parable of the sower, He described it this way:

> So is the kingdom of God, as if a man should cast seed into the ground; and should sleep, and rise night and day, and the seed should spring and grow up, he knoweth not how. For the earth bringeth forth fruit of herself; first the blade, then the ear, after that the full corn in the ear. But when the fruit is brought forth, immediately he putteth in the sickle, because the harvest is come (Mark 4:26-29).

Notice, you don't get out your sickle and try to start reaping the moment the first little blade of faith appears. You have to be patient and let The WORD finish its work. You have to wait for your faith crop to ripen.

As you do, you'll begin to see the thing you're believing for more clearly with the eyes of your heart. You'll start getting some confirmations and revelations from The LORD about it. He'll begin to show you where that property is you've been standing in faith for. He'll show you the building...or the house...or whatever else you've been claiming according to His WORD.

When those things start to happen, it's exciting. But it's also a time when you must stay full of faith that THE BLESSING is working in your life. You must continue to be patient and keep believing it's working—when you see it and when you don't, when you feel it and when you don't. You have to stay

steady and on track because the devil will do everything he can to push you into getting out ahead of God and trying to make something happen too early. He'll work hard to pressure you into eating your crop while it's still green.

A lot of people do that, and it's a serious mistake. That's how people end up in financial trouble. They try to buy the building or the house or the car God promised them before it's time, instead of waiting to find out from Him exactly how He wants to get it to them.

Every one of us has done that at one time or another. We can all remember the bitter taste of green corn. But, personally, I don't want to make a steady diet of it. So I asked The LORD one day, "How can we know for sure when our harvest is ripe?"

I have put in the heart of every human being an awesome sense of timing, He said. *They have an innate ability to know when something is right.*

I recognized right away just how true that is. People who have never even been on a farm can go to a grocery store and tell immediately what's ripe and what's not. They won't eat fruit that's been picked before it's ready, unless that's all they have to eat, because it just doesn't taste good.

One way we know something is ripe is when it just falls off the tree. That's true in the natural and the spirit realm. When the time for your faith harvest has come, things just start working. Circumstances fall miraculously into line. People just start doing their best to help you in that area. It becomes obvious: THE BLESSING has done its work, and harvest time is here.

NOTES

NOTES

It's Time to Reap Your Harvest!

DAY 10

A. Series Review

   1.   The Missing Link

      a.   Concerning EMIC's giving, Keith Moore said, "God's heart is grieved. It is bothering God that we are not reaping. I challenge you to hear the word of the Lord and make up your mind and say, 'I am not just a good giver. I am a good reaper. I am going to get real good at reaping.'"
—Keith Moore, Sept. 28, 1999

      b.   Reaping became the missing link to our increase.

      c.   Result: We have become much better reapers.

   2.   We were created by God to reap harvest.

   3.   Rules of Reaping

      a.   Reaping is not automatic.

      b.   Reaping is our responsibility.

      c.   Reaping requires faith.

   4.   The connection between tithing and reaping

   5.   The connection between sowing and reaping

   6.   Three essentials for a great harvest:

      a.   Expect your seed to grow.

      b.   Water your seed.

      c.   Keep the weeds out.

7. A good harvester knows:
   a. When to reap
   b. Where to reap
   c. To reap it all

B. Isaiah 41:15—It's Time to Reap Your Harvest!

1. Behold, I will make thee a new sharp threshing instrument having teeth: thou shalt thresh the mountains, and beat them small, and shalt make the hills as chaff.

2. *Teeth* (HEB) = mouths

3. We reap our harvest the same way we acquire anything else—by faith.

4. Our words of faith bring in the harvest.

5. Romans 4:17—Call those things which be not as though they were.
   a. *Call* (GK) = summons, command, demand
   b. Summon your harvest to come to you.

C. Father, by faith we command our harvest to come to us right now. We believe we reap the hundredfold return harvest from our sowing. Satan, take your hands off of our harvest. Angels, go get it and bring it to us! We reap it by faith in Jesus' Name. We are getting "real good at reaping"!

I will send you the seasonal rains. The land will then yield its crops, and the trees of the field will produce their fruit. Your threshing season will overlap with the grape harvest, and your grape harvest will overlap with the season of planting grain. You will eat your fill and live securely in your own land.

—Leviticus 26:4-5, NLT

You will have such a surplus of crops that you will need to clear out the old grain to make room for the new harvest!

—Leviticus 26:10, NLT

You will still be eating last year's harvest when you will have to move it out to make room for the new.

—Leviticus 26:10, NIV

NOTES

NOTES

HOW TO REAP YOUR HARVEST

BY PASTOR GEORGE PEARSONS

It was a word I was not expecting.

The date was Sept. 28, 1999, and Brother Keith Moore was our guest speaker at church. He stepped up to the podium and began to declare a word from the Lord for our congregation.

At first, I was stunned.

Through Brother Keith, the Lord let us know He was blessed by our giving, but He was grieved and bothered that we weren't reaping.

> "The Lord let us know **He was blessed by our giving**, but He was grieved and bothered that we weren't reaping."

Ouch!

Through Brother Keith, the Lord informed us that some were disillusioned and aggravated with Him, and asking, "How much more can I give?"

But here was the clincher. The Lord said, *You think you are waiting on Me. You think reaping is automatic. You think that once you put the money in, it's all up to Me. That is ignorance and confusion. I challenge you to hear the word of the Lord and make up your mind and say, "I am not just a good giver. I am a good reaper. And I am going to get real good at reaping!"*

That night, I took His challenge seriously.

I determined that we were going to get "real good" at reaping.

The first thing I did was to order a teaching series by Brother Moore titled *Rules of Reaping.* I listened to those messages over and over. I took copious

notes and looked up every scripture. Within one month, I taught a three-day seminar based on his messages.

From that moment on, my life and the life of our church began to change. This word revolutionized our thinking. Reaping our harvest was the missing link—a major key that unlocked the door to increase. Every time we received the offering, we would call in our harvest. We were determined to get *real good* at reaping.

➜ REAPING IS NOT AUTOMATIC ❦

Consider the farmer who invests time and money planting a crop. Then, at harvest time, he simply sits on the porch and watches it rot in the field. Our response would be, "That's crazy!" Unfortunately, that is the way some Christians think. Too many are sleeping through their harvest. Proverbs 10:5 in the *New Living Translation* says, "A wise youth harvests in the summer, but one who sleeps during harvest is a disgrace." Many sow their seed and then just wait for God to reap the harvest. That is not the way it works. A natural harvest doesn't just jump from the field into the barn. Someone must go out and reap it. And that someone is us!

> "A natural harvest doesn't just jump from the field into the barn. Someone must go out and reap it. **And that someone is us!**"

Mark 4:26-29 confirms that reaping is our responsibility. Jesus said, "So is the kingdom of God, as if a man should cast seed into the ground; and should sleep, and rise night and day, and the seed should spring and grow up, he knoweth not how. For the earth bringeth forth fruit of herself; first the blade, then the ear, after that the full corn in the ear. But when the fruit is brought forth, immediately he putteth in the sickle, because the harvest is come."

I know you weren't expecting it, but here's a pop quiz on what you just read. And so you'll pass with flying colors, I'm giving you the answers.

1. Who did the sowing? (Man)
2. Who did the growing? (God)
3. Who reaped the harvest? (Man)

In the July 9 installment of Kenneth and Gloria Copeland's daily devotional *From Faith to Faith,* Brother Copeland writes, "Jesus compared the kingdom of God with the planting of seed and reaping the harvest. It's a simple concept. One all of us understand. Why, then, aren't all of us producing bumper crops every season? Because we are sitting around waiting for God to do all the work."

❧ WE WERE CREATED TO REAP ❧

Earlier this year, Gloria Copeland and I spent two weeks on the *Believer's Voice of Victory* broadcast teaching on the topic "How to Reap Your Harvest." If you missed any of those teachings from last May, I encourage you to visit the KCM website, find those 10 days of broadcasts in the archives section and watch them. They will help renew your mind to the importance of reaping your harvest.

During the taping, Gloria and I were discussing the fact that God created Adam to harvest. Genesis 2:15 says, "And the Lord God took the man, and put him into the garden of Eden to dress it and to keep it." That definitely included sowing and reaping. We read Genesis 8:22, and determined that sowing and reaping have not passed away. "While the earth remaineth, *seedtime and harvest,* and cold and heat, and summer and winter, and day and night shall not cease."

Then, Gloria said something I had never heard before.

She declared, "We *still* have a 'harvest gene.' It's in our DNA."

God created us to harvest. That is what THE BLESSING has empowered

us to do. We still have what it takes to reap the harvest from every good seed we sow.

Here is another example. Look at Matthew 6:26. "Behold the fowls of the air: for they sow not, neither do they reap, nor gather into barns; yet your heavenly Father feedeth them. Are ye not much better than they?"

While meditating on this scripture, I asked the Lord why we were better than birds. Without hesitation, He answered. *Because you were created to sow and reap, and they weren't.* Think of it! You and I were created by God to sow our seed, reap our harvest and gather it into barns. But, don't ever forget our purpose for reaping: Our motivation for accumulation is distribution.

❧ HOW TO REAP YOUR HARVEST ❧

I once heard about a preacher who was struggling financially. Physically, he was well and strong. He experienced powerful demonstrations of the spirit in his meetings, and his ministry was growing rapidly. The only area of trouble was in the financial realm. Even though he was a tither and a sower, he was not seeing the financial results he desired and needed. He decided to fast and pray. He sought the Lord to find out why he was having such financial difficulty. As a result of his time of separation, the Lord told him he had to receive his finances the same way he received his healing—by faith. In other words, He told him to "call in the harvest."

"We *still* have a 'harvest gene.' **It's in our DNA.**" —❮❮❮❮❮

How do we do that? We call in the harvest with our words of faith.

Isaiah 41:15 says, "I will make thee a new sharp threshing instrument having teeth." The word *teeth* in the Hebrew is the word *mouths.* Our mouths are designed by God to be mighty combines—huge threshing machines that go into the field and bring in the harvest.

Gloria said something else during the broadcast concerning the difference between a natural harvest and a spiritual harvest. She said that a natural harvest is seasonal. It all depends on the weather cycle. A spiritual harvest, on the other hand, is continual. A spiritual harvest does not depend on the weather or the economy. It's year-round!

> ## "A spiritual harvest does not depend on the weather or the economy. It's year-round!"

The kingdom of God is always on the increase in spite of contrary conditions. Read Jeremiah 17:7-8. "Blessed is the man that trusteth in the Lord, and whose hope the Lord is. For he shall be as a tree planted by the waters, and that spreadeth out her roots by the river, and shall not see when heat cometh, but her leaf shall be green; and shall not be careful in the year of drought, *neither shall cease from yielding fruit.*"

We can actually come to a place in our lives where we are reaping all the time. "'The time will come,'" says the Lord, "'when the grain and grapes will grow faster than they can be harvested'" (Amos 9:13, *New Living Translation*).

❧ THINK HARVEST! ❧

Consider what Brother Copeland said several years ago in an article he wrote, titled "Get Your Mind on the Harvest." He said, "If you haven't thought of yourself as a harvester before now, start thinking of yourself that way. Renew your mind to the truth of God's WORD. Dare to believe The LORD of the Harvest is calling you—yes, *you*—to help Him bring in His end time crops. He's speaking to you and saying, 'Until now, you've known Me as The LORD over your seed. You've known Me as your bread provider. But, I want you to know Me now as LORD and Minister of the Harvest.'"

Harvester, don't wait one more minute. Open your mouth—your spiritual combine—and call in your harvest. As Joel 3:13 says, "Swing the sickle—the harvest is ready" (*The Message*).

"Father, I commit to be a good sower *and* a good reaper. I see in Your Word that harvesting is my responsibility. By my words of faith, I *will* reap my full harvest from the seed I have sown. Harvest, I command you to come to me. I refuse to back off and get discouraged. I will stay strong in faith. I take my hundredfold return harvest. Satan, take your hands off my harvest. Angels, go get it and bring it to me in Jesus' Name!"

Praise God! We are not just good givers. We are good reapers. And, together, we are getting *real good* at reaping!

GET YOUR MIND ON THE HARVEST

BY KENNETH COPELAND

If you've been sowing seed into the kingdom of God, I have news that will put a smile on your face, a skip in your step and joy in your heart.

Harvest time is here!

That's right. As the Body of Christ, we've stepped into the season we've all been waiting for. We've moved into the time when the spiritual and financial crops we've planted...and tended...and believed for are coming up. It's a time to rejoice and celebrate.

There's nothing better than the thrill of harvest time! Oral Roberts, my spiritual father, and Gloria and I were talking about that fact not long ago, because the Lord had been speaking to him about it. He'd been reminding Brother Roberts of the days back when he held tent meetings in farm communities.

Sometimes he'd come into towns where the crops had been reaped and sold at a good price, and the streets would be full of joyful people. Everyone would be smiling and shouting greetings to each other. They'd be busy buying school clothes for the kids and stocking up for the winter. It was a glorious scene.

I know from my own experience what that's like. As a child, I used to spend time on my grandfather's farm. When harvest time came, whole truck-loads of people would show up to help bring in the crops. All the kids would play together and at dinnertime, because there were too many people to fit into one house, the whole bunch of us would eat outside.

What fun that was! Everyone was making money. Everyone was on the move. Everyone was enjoying the fruits of their labor.

Nobody was thinking anymore about how hot and tired they'd been when they were out working in the fields, or talking about how their feet got

blistered and their hands got calloused when they were chopping cotton and hoeing weeds. They'd forgotten about all that.

They had their minds on the harvest!

"THERE'S NOTHING BETTER
than the thrill of harvest time!"

➜ MAKING THE SWITCH ❦

That's the way we, as seed-sowing believers, ought to be today. We should have our "reaping" faith in gear and our minds on the harvest.

That's a switch for a lot of us because until now, we've focused our faith primarily on planting. We've concentrated on God's promise to provide *seed to the sower* and *bread to the eater.*

Thank God for such bread-receiving, seed-sowing faith! It's wonderful. It's opened the door for God to meet our needs and give us enough to invest in the work of His kingdom. But that's not all God wants to do for us. He didn't just promise to give us food to eat and seed to sow, He promised to multiply that seed and give us a harvest. He said:

> He which soweth sparingly shall reap also sparingly; and he which soweth bountifully shall reap also bountifully. Every man accord-ing as he purposeth in his heart, so let him give; not grudgingly, or of necessity: for God loveth a cheerful giver. And God is able to make all grace abound toward you; that ye, always having all sufficiency in all things, may abound to every good work. (As it is written, He hath dispersed abroad; he hath given to the poor: his righteousness remaineth for ever. Now he that ministereth seed to the sower both minister bread for your food, and multiply your seed sown, and increase the fruits of your righteousness;)

being enriched in every thing to all bountifulness, which causeth through us thanksgiving to God (2 Corinthians 9:6-11).

God has had harvest time in His sights all along. That's why He taught us about sowing and reaping. That's why He sustained us and met our needs while we were waiting for our crops to come up. He intended to multiply our seed and give us such abundant harvests that we'd always have all sufficiency in all things and wouldn't need any outside aid or support.

> "From the very beginning, **God's aim** was to **bless us so extravagantly** that we could demonstrate to the world that **we don't need anyone but Jesus** to support us."

From the very beginning, God's aim was to bless us so extravagantly that we could demonstrate to the world that we don't need anyone but Jesus to support us. He is our Source. He is the One who enriches us in all things. He is the Lord of the Harvest!

❧ MORE THAN WE EXPECTED ❧

Jesus *is* the Lord of the Harvest. He called Himself that in Luke 10:2. When He sent His disciples out two-by-two into the cities of Israel, He said, "The harvest truly is great, but the labourers are few: pray ye therefore the Lord of the harvest, that he would send forth labourers into his harvest."

The problem is, many believers haven't exercised their faith in the harvest aspect of Jesus' ministry. They've gotten stuck instead on the seed-sowing part. "Brother Copeland," they say, "I just keep sowing...and sowing...and sowing but nothing is happening."

Sometimes they even complain about what happened to their seed after they planted it. "I gave $50 to a minister, and then I saw his son riding around on a new bike. I don't think he should have spent my money that way!"

"...the harvest **this generation of believers** is reaping is far greater than we ever expected."

People with that attitude are digging up their seed. They're interrupting the growth process and killing their crop. When Brother Roberts told us what God was showing him about harvest time, he said that's a mistake believers must stop making. He said we must all learn to sow our seed, release our faith, then forget about the seed.

Forget about it?

Yes, forget about it! Let it go! It's covered up in the soil of God's kingdom. We'll never see it again. So we should stop fussing over it...and worrying about it...and wondering what's become of it.

"Ken, get your mind off the sowing part now," he said, "and get it on the harvest instead!"

Ever since that discussion, I've been doing that more and more. In the process, the Lord has revealed some things to me. He's let me know, for instance, that the harvest this generation of believers is reaping is far greater than we ever expected. We are bringing in crops we didn't even plant.

How is that possible?

It's simple. Many believers in generations gone by who were faithful to sow seed into the kingdom of God didn't know anything about harvest. As a result, they didn't reap what belonged to them. They left their spiritual crops in the field.

For a long time, my mom and dad were like that. They had such a strong revelation of the importance of giving into God's kingdom that they actually added tithing to their wedding vows. Back in 1927 when they were married, they declared they would tithe every dollar that came into their hands all their married life.

They did it, too. All his adult life, my dad had two bank accounts: One

was God's and the other was his. He never mixed them up. As a young boy, I'd go with him to the bank and watch him make out two different deposit slips, one for each account. My dad was diligent to do that for many years. He didn't know how to reach out

"God never forgets a seed. He never counts it out. He always multiplies the seed sown, then He goes looking for someone with faith enough to harvest it."

and receive his harvest by faith, however, until much later in life. So he never received the fullness of what he'd planted.

Over the centuries, there have been many faithful tithers and givers like my dad—believers who sowed a lifetime of seeds and, because they knew nothing about reaping, never reaped the return. The devil thinks their seeds are buried and forgotten. But God never forgets a seed. He never counts it out. He always multiplies the seed sown, then He goes looking for someone with faith enough to harvest it.

And you know what? We're the generation of believers He's been looking for!

We're the ones who've been blessed with the last days outpouring of the Holy Spirit and the revelation of harvest. We're the ones who will reap the spiritual and financial crops sown by our grandfathers and grandmothers. We'll bring in harvests sown by spiritual ancestors we don't even know.

❧ DIFFERENT CROPS: THE SAME ANOINTING ❧

I start jumping every time I think about that because harvest time is a happy time. Harvest time is what makes all the work worthwhile. That's true in the natural scheme of things and it's even more true spiritually.

Think about it. What could possibly be more thrilling than reaping the biggest harvest of souls in the 2,000-year history of the Body of Christ?

I'm telling you by the Spirit of God, that's what we are doing. It's already started. More people are coming into the family of God than ever before in all of Christian history. The Lord of the Harvest is sending us out as laborers to gather up the most staggering spiritual crop this world has ever seen. This is the beginning of massive harvest!

"But Brother Copeland," someone might say, "I thought you were talking about a financial harvest. I thought you were saying the financial seeds we've sown are ready to be reaped."

I am.

You see, you can't have a spiritual harvest by itself. You have to have a financial harvest at the same time because harvest time is the most expensive season of the year.

I learned that in my boyhood days on my grandfather's farm. At harvest time, you're buying more fuel, you're hiring more people, you're spending everything you have to get that crop in from the field before the weather starts to ruin it.

That's why it takes a harvest of finances to reap a harvest of souls. Bringing in those spiritual sheaves is expensive! That's OK, though, because the same anointing that brings forth the spiritual crop brings forth the financial crop. Both kinds of seeds are multiplied by THE BLESSING that flows to us and through us from the Lord of the Harvest.

So, roll up your spiritual sleeves and go to work in both realms. Get ready to have the time of your life.

If you haven't thought of yourself as a harvester before now, start thinking of yourself that way. Renew your mind to the truth of

> "Both kinds of seeds are multiplied by **THE BLESSING** that flows to us and through us **from the Lord of the Harvest.**"

God's Word. Dare to believe the Lord of the Harvest is calling you—yes, *you!*—to help Him bring in His end-time crops. He's speaking to you and saying, "Until now, you've known Me as the Lord over your seed. You've known Me as your bread provider. But I want you to know Me now as Lord and Minister of the harvest."

❧ MYSTERIES REVEALED ❧

I'm persuaded that's what Jesus is saying to every believer who will listen these days. His fields are ripe and He is hunting high and low for those who will open their Bibles, stand on His promises of blessing, and get their harvest faith in gear. He is searching for bold receivers who won't back away in doubt, but will jump on the truck with the rest of the harvesters and head for the fields.

The Lord spoke by prophecy during the 2006 West Coast Believers' Convention and said those who respond in that way will be equipped with revelation that will help them get the job done. He said:

> *More and more, faster and faster, in more clarity and detail, the anointing will cause revelation to flow and mysteries in Christ to come clear as never before in these days in which you live. For these are the times when the mysteries shall be unveiled and you'll say, "My, my, isn't that simple, isn't that wonderful." Hallelujah. And it is and will continue to be that way because these are the times,* saith the Lord, *when* all *people will see the glory. The whole earth shall be filled with it. Amen. This is that day and this is that hour and for those that are committed, and those that are strong in the Word, and those that put My Word first place in their lives will continue to flow, and it will be a continuous flow of revelation in your life and it'll get sweeter and sweeter as the days go by. It's harvest time!*

Things are going to increase in intensity. There are those of you that will begin to experience an outflow and overflow not only of anointing to minister to people, but in the financial realm also. And the increase will come not because of more work, or more effort on your part, but because of the intensified flow of the Holy Ghost. Not by might, not by any other way except by My Spirit, saith the Lord. *My power and revelation of the love of God on a level and on a plane never before seen, never before understood by the general population of the Body of Jesus Christ.*

The revealings of the secrets of faith and power. Hallelujah. Glorified knowledge in the Holy Ghost, and how to walk in anointings that will cause people to receive Jesus as Lord and Savior; Jesus as Baptizer in the Holy Ghost; Jesus as Healer and Jesus as Financier. You will be able to help them receive on a much higher plane and it will seem like, "Why, this is just the most effortless thing I have ever seen," and that is exactly true. You are walking into an effortless, sweatless anointing. Hallelujah. A time of great outpouring. It's here, it's already in operation, saith the Lord. *So jump in, jump in and enjoy the swim for the time has come.*

Jesus is the High Priest and Chief Executive of heaven's finances, and it's harvest time in the kingdom of God!

REAPING A HARVEST OF HEALING

BY GLORIA COPELAND

The Bible teaches us in Mark, chapter 4, that the Word of God is seed. If you plant the seed of God's Word, you can reap a harvest of results; but you must plant the specific seed that you want. If you plant corn, you will reap corn. If you plant the Word for salvation in your heart, you will have faith to receive salvation. When you plant the Word concerning healing in your heart, you will reap the healing harvest.

First Peter 1:23 says, "Being born again, not of corruptible seed, but of incorruptible, by the word of God, which liveth and abideth for ever." The incorruptible Word is the seed that goes into the heart of man. God's Word cannot be corrupted. It cannot be spoiled by any power. When you heard that Jesus died for you and was raised from the dead, you decided to make Him your Lord because of the Word

> **"God's Word cannot be corrupted.** It cannot be spoiled by any power."

that you heard. When you made Jesus the Lord of your life, that incorruptible Word went into your heart and no satanic influence could stop it from producing results in your life. At that moment, you were born again.

Faith comes for healing in the same way it comes for salvation—by hearing the Word of God. There is no substitute for the seed of the Word. For a while, you can receive healing by having someone else pray for you, but ultimately you will have to plant your own crop in order to enjoy divine health. In the middle of the night when Satan attacks you with symptoms, there may

not be anyone there to pray for you. If you have taken the time to plant God's Word in your heart, then you will have that knowledge with you always.

A mistake many people have made is in trying to fit the Word into their own traditional ideas. In Mark 4:23 Jesus said, "If any man have ears to hear, let him hear." The *Amplified Bible, Classic Edition* says, "If any man has ears to hear, let him be listening, and perceive and comprehend." If you will listen to God and study the Word for yourself, you will receive the truth that will set you free. The respect that you give to the Word of God as being the authority will be the measure of virtue, or power, that comes back to you. If you will make a decision to do whatever you see in the Word and make God's Word the final authority in your life, then you will have the hundredfold principle of power working in you. Traditional ideas and teaching have kept the Body of Christ robbed of power. You would be helpless to receive healing if you didn't know it was God's will for you to be healed.

Many try to reap a healing harvest without first planting the seed. F.F. Bosworth says in his book, *Christ the Healer,* "Until the person seeking healing is sure from God's Word that it is God's will to heal him, he is trying to reap a harvest where there is no seed planted." He is like a farmer who sits on his porch and says, "I believe in cotton, so this year I'm going to sit here and believe for a harvest. I'm not going to plant any seed; I'm just going to believe for a harvest." He can sit there forever, but he will not reap a harvest until he plants the seed.

> "If you will make a decision to do whatever you see in the Word and **make God's Word the final authority in your life,** then you will have the hundredfold principle of power working in you."

You can do the same thing with healing. You can say, "I believe in healing. I know God heals." But if you don't go another step and say, "I believe that it's God's will to heal me," you will sit on the front porch and watch the healing

harvest go to somebody else. If you expect to get results, you have to believe that it's God's will to heal you.

God desires for you to be healed and whole. In fact, He desires for you to walk in divine health. You need to allow revelation knowledge of divine health to become a reality in your life. For years, Kenneth and I were believers. We believed in healing. We knew it was real. When we got sick, we would pray. Sometimes we got healed; sometimes we would stay sick. But then one night we heard that healing had already been bought and paid for us by Jesus. When we heard that, we knew that our days of sickness were over. We received God's Word and that seed bore fruit in our spirits instantly. It doesn't take God's Word long to bear fruit. If it is planted on good ground and you take heed to what you hear, you can plant the crop and reap a harvest of

— ≪≪≪≪ **"It doesn't take God's Word long to bear fruit."**

healing quickly. From the day we heard of the substitution of Jesus Christ for our sicknesses and diseases, sickness absolutely lost all power over us.

When the seed of God's Word becomes real to you in your spirit concerning your healing, that Word will produce healing in your life.

Matthew 8:17 says, "That it might be fulfilled which was spoken by Esaias the prophet, saying, Himself took our infirmities, and bare our sicknesses." You have a choice here: You can take heed to what you hear or you can write it off. If you want results, you will listen to what you hear and believe this Word more than anything else you have been told. When Jesus bore our sins, He also bore our sicknesses and disease. The Cross produced a double cure for the ills of mankind. Jesus came to destroy the works of the devil—all of them! He couldn't take away sin and leave sickness. Jesus destroyed the curse and everything it involved. He stripped Satan and left him powerless, with nothing but deception.

Allow God's Word to be planted in your heart and your days of sickness will be over! The light of God's Word will destroy Satan's grip in your life. The

truth will make you free from his dominion when you realize that your healing has already been purchased by Jesus. The Word

"The **light of God's Word** will destroy Satan's grip in your life."

says, "By his stripes, you were healed." That is not a promise. That is a fact! The work has already been done. Your healing has already been provided for you.

The only thing left is for you to make the decision to live in divine health. Refuse to allow any sickness to stay in your body.

Determine today to make the decision to live in health and healing. God wants His people well. He wants you well and whole! He has provided His incorruptible Word as the avenue for you to receive your health and healing. Have the determination of faith to enjoy all that Jesus has provided for you. He was made sick with your sicknesses. You don't have to bear them.

Make this confession of faith before God:

"Father, in the Name of Jesus, I have accepted Jesus as my Lord and Savior, so now I accept Him as my healer. I say now with my mouth that my body is healed—from the top of my head to the tips of my toes. I determine now to walk in the light of healing in my spirit, in my mind, and in my body. I believe that just as surely as Jesus bore my sins, He also bore my sicknesses. I stand now, in Jesus' Name, and proclaim that I am free from the bondage of Satan."

If you have sickness in your body right now, then speak to it now:

"Sickness, I resist you in Jesus' Name. I refuse to allow you in my body any longer. I command you to leave. Satan, you'll not lord it over me. In Jesus' Name, your work has been destroyed!"

Now rejoice in what God has already done for you through Jesus and what He is continuing to do in you at this moment! Praise God!